Cram101 Textbook Outlines to accompany:

Diversity in Early Care and Education: Honoring Differences

Gonzalez-Mena, 5th Edition

An Academic Internet Publishers (AIPI) publication (c) 2007.

Cram101 and Cram101.com are AIPI publications and services. All notes, highlights, reviews, and practice tests are prepared by AIPI for use in AIPI publications, all rights reserved.

You have a discounted membership at www.Cram101.com with this book.

Get all of the practice tests for the chapters of this textbook, and access in-depth reference material for writing essays and papers. Here is an example from a Cram101 Biology text:

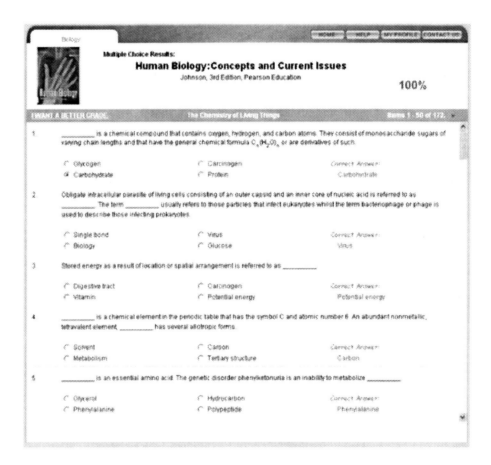

When you need problem solving help with math, stats, and other disciplines, www.Cram101.com will walk through the formulas and solutions step by step.

With Cram101.com online, you also have access to extensive reference material.

You will nail those essays and papers. Here is an example from a Cram101 Biology text:

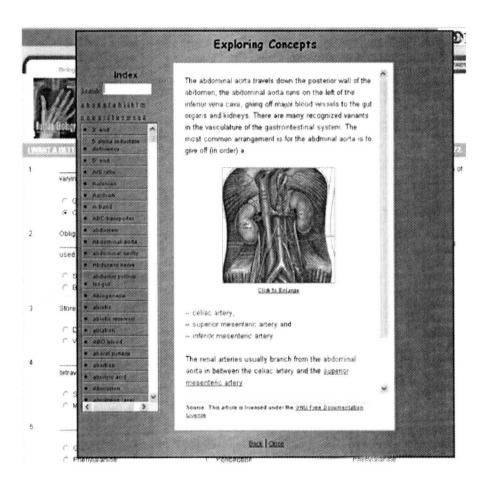

Visit **www.Cram101.com**, click Sign Up at the top of the screen, and enter DK73DW3659 in the promo code box on the registration screen. Access to www.Cram101.com is normally $9.95, but because you have purchased this book, your access fee is only $4.95. Sign up and stop highlighting textbooks forever.

Learning System

Cram101 Textbook Outlines is a learning system. The notes in this book are the highlights of your textbook, you will never have to highlight a book again.

How to use this book. Take this book to class, it is your notebook for the lecture. The notes and highlights on the left hand side of the pages follow the outline and order of the textbook. All you have to do is follow along while your intructor presents the lecture. Circle the items emphasized in class and add other important information on the right side. With Cram101 Textbook Outlines you'll spend less time writing and more time listening. Learning becomes more efficient.

Cram101.com Online

Increase your studying efficiency by using Cram101.com's practice tests and online reference material. It is the perfect complement to Cram101 Textbook Outlines. Use self-teaching matching tests or simulate in-class testing with comprehensive multiple choice tests, or simply use Cram's true and false tests for quick review. Cram101.com even allows you to enter your in-class notes for an integrated studying format combining the textbook notes with your class notes.

Visit **www.Cram101.com**, click Sign Up at the top of the screen, and enter **DK73DW3659** in the promo code box on the registration screen. Access to www.Cram101.com is normally $9.95, but because you have purchased this book, your access fee is only $4.95. Sign up and stop highlighting textbooks forever.

Copyright © 2008 by Academic Internet Publishers, Inc. All rights reserved. "Cram101"® and "Never Highlight a Book Again!"® are registered trademarks of Academic Internet Publishers, Inc. The Cram101 Textbook Outline series is printed in the United States. ISBN(s): 1-4288-2090-6 perfect-bound, and 1-4288-2091-4 spiral bound.

Diversity in Early Care and Education: Honoring Differences
Gonzalez-Mena, 5th

CONTENTS

1. Perceiving and Responding to Differences 2
2. Communicating across Cultures 6
3. Working with Diversity Issues 10
4. A Framework for Understanding Differences 14
5. Attachment and Separation 18
6. Differing Perspectives on Learning through Play 22
7. Socialization, Guidance, and Discipline 26

Chapter 1. Perceiving and Responding to Differences

Lesbian	A lesbian is a homosexual woman. They are women who are sexually and romantically attracted to other women.
Attitude	An enduring mental representation of a person, place, or thing that evokes an emotional response and related behavior is called attitude.
Attention	Attention is the cognitive process of selectively concentrating on one thing while ignoring other things. Psychologists have labeled three types of attention: sustained attention, selective attention, and divided attention.
Early childhood	Early childhood refers to the developmental period extending from the end of infancy to about 5 or 6 years of age; sometimes called the preschool years.
Norms	In testing, standards of test performance that permit the comparison of one person's score on the test to the scores of others who have taken the same test are referred to as norms.
Child development	Scientific study of the processes of change from conception through adolescence is called child development.
Pluralism	Pluralism refers to the coexistence of distinct ethnic and cultural groups in the same society. Individuals with a pluralistic stance usually advocate that cultural differences be maintained and appreciated.
Developmentally disabled	developmentally disabled is a term for a pattern of persistently slow learning of basic motor and language skills during childhood, and a significantly below-normal global intellectual capacity as an adult.
Nonverbal communication	Communication between individuals that does not involve the content of spoken language, but relies instead on an unspoken language of facial expressions, eye contact, and body language is nonverbal communication.
Personality	Personality refers to the pattern of enduring characteristics that differentiates a person, the patterns of behaviors that make each individual unique.
Affect	A subjective feeling or emotional tone often accompanied by bodily expressions noticeable to others is called affect.
Learning	Learning is a relatively permanent change in behavior that results from experience. Thus, to attribute a behavioral change to learning, the change must be relatively permanent and must result from experience.
Stereotype	A stereotype is considered to be a group concept, held by one social group about another. They are often used in a negative or prejudicial sense and are frequently used to justify certain discriminatory behaviors. This allows powerful social groups to legitimize and protect their dominant position
Infancy	The developmental period that extends from birth to 18 or 24 months is called infancy.
Synchrony	In child development, synchrony is the carefully coordinated interaction between the parent and the child or adolescent in which, often unknowingly, they are attuned to each other's behavior.
Connectedness	Connectedness, according to Cooper, consists of two dimensions: mutuality and permeability. Connectedness involves processes that link the self to others, as seen in acknowledgment of, respect for, and responsiveness to others.
Sexism	Sexism is commonly considered to be discrimination against people based on their sex rather than their individual merits, but can also refer to any and all differentiations based on sex.
Bias	A bias is a prejudice in a general or specific sense, usually in the sense for having a preference to one particular point of view or ideological perspective.
Authoritarian	The term authoritarian is used to describe a style that enforces strong and sometimes oppressive measures against those in its sphere of influence, generally without attempts at gaining their consent.

Chapter 1. Perceiving and Responding to Differences

Chapter 1. Perceiving and Responding to Differences

Ambivalence	The simultaneous holding of strong positive and negative emotional attitudes toward the same situation or person is called ambivalence.
Toddler	A toddler is a child between the ages of one and three years old. During this period, the child learns a great deal about social roles and develops motor skills; to toddle is to walk unsteadily.
Problem solving	An attempt to find an appropriate way of attaining a goal when the goal is not readily available is called problem solving.
Context	In Psychology, context refers to the background stimuli that accompany some kind of foreground event.
Generalization	In conditioning, the tendency for a conditioned response to be evoked by stimuli that are similar to the stimulus to which the response was conditioned is a generalization. The greater the similarity among the stimuli, the greater the probability of generalization.
Social class	Social class describes the relationships between people in hierarchical societies or cultures. Those with more power usually subordinate those with less power.
Socialization	Social rules and social relations are created, communicated, and changed in verbal and nonverbal ways creating social complexity useful in identifying outsiders and intelligent breeding partners. The process of learning these skills is called socialization.
Individualism	Individualism refers to putting personal goals ahead of group goals and defining one's identity in terms of personal attributes rather than group memberships.
Ecology	Ecology refers to the branch of biology that deals with the relationships between living organisms and their environment.
Bronfenbrenner	Bronfenbrenner was a co-founder of the U.S. national Head Start program and founder of the Ecological Theory of Development.
Interdependence	Interdependence is a dynamic of being mutually responsible to and dependent on others.
Anchor	An anchor is a sample of work or performance used to set the specific performance standard for a rubric level.
Society	The social sciences use the term society to mean a group of people that form a semi-closed (or semi-open) social system, in which most interactions are with other individuals belonging to the group.
Developmental psychology	The branch of psychology that studies the patterns of growth and change occurring throughout life is referred to as developmental psychology.
Pedagogy	Pedagogy is the art or science of teaching. The word comes from the ancient Greek paidagogos, the slave who took children to and from school.

Go to **Cram101.com** for the Practice Tests for this Chapter.

Chapter 1. Perceiving and Responding to Differences

Chapter 2. Communicating across Cultures

Statistic	A statistic is an observable random variable of a sample.
Statistics	Statistics is a type of data analysis which practice includes the planning, summarizing, and interpreting of observations of a system possibly followed by predicting or forecasting of future events based on a mathematical model of the system being observed.
Learning	Learning is a relatively permanent change in behavior that results from experience. Thus, to attribute a behavioral change to learning, the change must be relatively permanent and must result from experience.
Population	Population refers to all members of a well-defined group of organisms, events, or things.
Cultural diversity	Cultural diversity is the variety of human societies or cultures in a specific region, or in the world as a whole.
Attitude	An enduring mental representation of a person, place, or thing that evokes an emotional response and related behavior is called attitude.
Maslow	Maslow is mostly noted today for his proposal of a hierarchy of human needs which he often presented as a pyramid. Maslow was an instrumental player in the formation of the humanistic movement, also known as the third force in psychology.
Humanistic	Humanistic refers to any system of thought focused on subjective experience and human problems and potentials.
Humanistic psychology	Humanistic psychology refers to the school of psychology that focuses on the uniqueness of human beings and their capacity for choice, growth, and psychological health.
Affect	A subjective feeling or emotional tone often accompanied by bodily expressions noticeable to others is called affect.
Human nature	Human nature is the fundamental nature and substance of humans, as well as the range of human behavior that is believed to be invariant over long periods of time and across very different cultural contexts.
Proxemics	The term proxemics was introduced by anthropologist Edward Hall in 1963 to describe the measureable distances between people as they interacted.
Personal space	Personal space is the region surrounding each person, or that area which a person considers his domain or territory. Often if entered by another being without this being desired, it makes them feel uncomfortable.
Attention	Attention is the cognitive process of selectively concentrating on one thing while ignoring other things. Psychologists have labeled three types of attention: sustained attention, selective attention, and divided attention.
Child abuse	Child abuse is the physical or psychological maltreatment of a child.
Feedback	Feedback refers to information returned to a person about the effects a response has had.
Personality	Personality refers to the pattern of enduring characteristics that differentiates a person, the patterns of behaviors that make each individual unique.
Questionnaire	A self-report method of data collection or clinical assessment method in which the individual being studied checks off items on a printed list, answers multiple-choice questions, or writes out answers to essay questions aimed at producing a selfdescription is called questionnaire.
Ethnicity	Ethnicity refers to a characteristic based on cultural heritage, nationality characteristics, race, religion, and language.
Bias	A bias is a prejudice in a general or specific sense, usually in the sense for having a

Chapter 2. Communicating across Cultures

Chapter 2. Communicating across Cultures

	preference to one particular point of view or ideological perspective.
Blind spot	In anatomy, the blind spot is the region of the retina where the optic nerve and blood vessels pass through to connect to the back of the eye. Since there are no light receptors there, a part of the field of vision is not perceived.
Insight	Insight refers to a sudden awareness of the relationships among various elements that had previously appeared to be independent of one another.
Early childhood	Early childhood refers to the developmental period extending from the end of infancy to about 5 or 6 years of age; sometimes called the preschool years.
Toddler	A toddler is a child between the ages of one and three years old. During this period, the child learns a great deal about social roles and develops motor skills; to toddle is to walk unsteadily.
Counselor	A counselor is a mental health professional who specializes in helping people with problems not involving serious mental disorders.
Anchor	An anchor is a sample of work or performance used to set the specific performance standard for a rubric level.

Go to **Cram101.com** for the Practice Tests for this Chapter.

Chapter 2. Communicating across Cultures

Chapter 3. Working with Diversity Issues

Emotion	An emotion is a mental states that arise spontaneously, rather than through conscious effort. They are often accompanied by physiological changes.
Learning	Learning is a relatively permanent change in behavior that results from experience. Thus, to attribute a behavioral change to learning, the change must be relatively permanent and must result from experience.
Attention	Attention is the cognitive process of selectively concentrating on one thing while ignoring other things. Psychologists have labeled three types of attention: sustained attention, selective attention, and divided attention.
Individualism	Individualism refers to putting personal goals ahead of group goals and defining one's identity in terms of personal attributes rather than group memberships.
Collectivism	Collectivism is an emphasis on the group, as opposed to the individual. It is syndrome of attitudes and behaviors based on the belief that the basic unit of survival lies within a group, not the individual.
Collectivist	A person who defines the self in terms of relationships to other people and groups and gives priority to group goals is called collectivist.
Evolution	Commonly used to refer to gradual change, evolution is the change in the frequency of alleles within a population from one generation to the next. This change may be caused by different mechanisms, including natural selection, genetic drift, or changes in population (gene flow).
Interdependence	Interdependence is a dynamic of being mutually responsible to and dependent on others.
Society	The social sciences use the term society to mean a group of people that form a semi-closed (or semi-open) social system, in which most interactions are with other individuals belonging to the group.
Developmentally appropriate practice	Education that focuses on the typical developmental patterns of children and the uniqueness of each child is called developmentally appropriate practice.
Child development	Scientific study of the processes of change from conception through adolescence is called child development.
Ethnocentrism	Ethnocentrism is the tendency to look at the world primarily from the perspective of one's own culture.
Problem solving	An attempt to find an appropriate way of attaining a goal when the goal is not readily available is called problem solving.
Affect	A subjective feeling or emotional tone often accompanied by bodily expressions noticeable to others is called affect.
Context	In Psychology, context refers to the background stimuli that accompany some kind of foreground event.
Stereotype	A stereotype is considered to be a group concept, held by one social group about another. They are often used in a negative or prejudicial sense and are frequently used to justify certain discriminatory behaviors. This allows powerful social groups to legitimize and protect their dominant position
Early childhood	Early childhood refers to the developmental period extending from the end of infancy to about 5 or 6 years of age; sometimes called the preschool years.
Epilepsy	Epilepsy is a chronic neurological condition characterized by recurrent unprovoked neural discharges. It is commonly controlled with medication, although surgical methods are used as well.

Go to **Cram101.com** for the Practice Tests for this Chapter.

Chapter 3. Working with Diversity Issues

Chapter 3. Working with Diversity Issues

Anchor	An anchor is a sample of work or performance used to set the specific performance standard for a rubric level.

Chapter 3. Working with Diversity Issues

Chapter 4. A Framework for Understanding Differences

Attitude	An enduring mental representation of a person, place, or thing that evokes an emotional response and related behavior is called attitude.
Individualist	A person who defines the self in terms of personal traits and gives priority to personal goals is an individualist.
Collectivist	A person who defines the self in terms of relationships to other people and groups and gives priority to group goals is called collectivist.
Collectivism	Collectivism is an emphasis on the group, as opposed to the individual. It is syndrome of attitudes and behaviors based on the belief that the basic unit of survival lies within a group, not the individual.
Early childhood	Early childhood refers to the developmental period extending from the end of infancy to about 5 or 6 years of age; sometimes called the preschool years.
Individuality	According to Cooper, individuality consists of two dimensions: self-assertion and separateness.
Interdependence	Interdependence is a dynamic of being mutually responsible to and dependent on others.
Autonomy	Autonomy is the condition of something that does not depend on anything else.
Individualism	Individualism refers to putting personal goals ahead of group goals and defining one's identity in terms of personal attributes rather than group memberships.
Attention	Attention is the cognitive process of selectively concentrating on one thing while ignoring other things. Psychologists have labeled three types of attention: sustained attention, selective attention, and divided attention.
Individualistic	Cultures have been classified as individualistic, which means having a set of values that give priority to personal goals rather than group goals.
Perception	Perception is the process of acquiring, interpreting, selecting, and organizing sensory information.
Learning	Learning is a relatively permanent change in behavior that results from experience. Thus, to attribute a behavioral change to learning, the change must be relatively permanent and must result from experience.
Obesity	The state of being more than 20 percent above the average weight for a person of one's height is called obesity.
Society	The social sciences use the term society to mean a group of people that form a semi-closed (or semi-open) social system, in which most interactions are with other individuals belonging to the group.
Modeling	A type of behavior learned through observation of others demonstrating the same behavior is modeling.
Attachment	Attachment is the tendency to seek closeness to another person and feel secure when that person is present.
Wisdom	Wisdom is the ability to make correct judgments and decisions. It is an intangible quality gained through experience. Whether or not something is wise is determined in a pragmatic sense by its popularity, how long it has been around, and its ability to predict against future events.
Toddler	A toddler is a child between the ages of one and three years old. During this period, the child learns a great deal about social roles and develops motor skills; to toddle is to walk unsteadily.

Chapter 4. A Framework for Understanding Differences

Chapter 4. A Framework for Understanding Differences

Malnutrition	Malnutrition is a general term for the medical condition in a person or animal caused by an unbalanced diet—either too little or too much food, or a diet missing one or more important nutrients.
Connectedness	Connectedness, according to Cooper, consists of two dimensions: mutuality and permeability. Connectedness involves processes that link the self to others, as seen in acknowledgment of, respect for, and responsiveness to others.
Script	A schema, or behavioral sequence, for an event is called a script. It is a form of schematic organization, with real-world events organized in terms of temporal and causal relations between component acts.
Child development	Scientific study of the processes of change from conception through adolescence is called child development.
Social class	Social class describes the relationships between people in hierarchical societies or cultures. Those with more power usually subordinate those with less power.
Ethnography	Ethnography is a holistic research method founded in the idea that a system's properties cannot necessarily be accurately understood independently of each other.
Spock	Spock was an American pediatrician whose book Baby and Child Care, published in 1946, is one of the biggest best-sellers of all time. Its revolutionary message to mothers was that "you know more than you think you do." Spock was the first pediatrician to study psychoanalysis to try to understand children's needs and family dynamics.
Multicultural perspective	A multicultural perspective focuses on understanding the cultural and ethnic factors that influence social behavior.
Adaptation	Adaptation is a lowering of sensitivity to a stimulus following prolonged exposure to that stimulus. Behavioral adaptations are special ways a particular organism behaves to survive in its natural habitat.

Chapter 4. A Framework for Understanding Differences

Chapter 5. Attachment and Separation

Attachment	Attachment is the tendency to seek closeness to another person and feel secure when that person is present.
Attention	Attention is the cognitive process of selectively concentrating on one thing while ignoring other things. Psychologists have labeled three types of attention: sustained attention, selective attention, and divided attention.
Stroke	A stroke occurs when the blood supply to a part of the brain is suddenly interrupted by occlusion, by hemorrhage, or other causes
Individualism	Individualism refers to putting personal goals ahead of group goals and defining one's identity in terms of personal attributes rather than group memberships.
Individualist	A person who defines the self in terms of personal traits and gives priority to personal goals is an individualist.
Personality	Personality refers to the pattern of enduring characteristics that differentiates a person, the patterns of behaviors that make each individual unique.
Population	Population refers to all members of a well-defined group of organisms, events, or things.
Infant mortality	Infant mortality is the death of infants in the first year of life. The leading causes of infant mortality are dehydration and disease. Major causes of infant mortality in more developed countries include congenital malformation, infection and SIDS. Infant mortality rate is the number of newborns dying under a year of age divided by the number of live births during the year.
Feedback	Feedback refers to information returned to a person about the effects a response has had.
Collectivist	A person who defines the self in terms of relationships to other people and groups and gives priority to group goals is called collectivist.
Collectivism	Collectivism is an emphasis on the group, as opposed to the individual. It is syndrome of attitudes and behaviors based on the belief that the basic unit of survival lies within a group, not the individual.
Cultural values	The importance and desirability of various objects and activities as defined by people in a given culture are referred to as cultural values.
Interdependence	Interdependence is a dynamic of being mutually responsible to and dependent on others.
Early childhood	Early childhood refers to the developmental period extending from the end of infancy to about 5 or 6 years of age; sometimes called the preschool years.
Bowlby	Bowlby, a developmental psychologist of the psychoanalytic tradition, was responsible for much of the early research conducted on attachment in humans. He identified three stages of separation: protest, despair, and detachment.
Attachment theory	Attachment theory is a theory about the psychological tendency to seek closeness to another person and feel secure when that person is present. A criticism of the theory is that it ignores the diversity of socializing agents and contexts that exists.
Toddler	A toddler is a child between the ages of one and three years old. During this period, the child learns a great deal about social roles and develops motor skills; to toddle is to walk unsteadily.
Anchor	An anchor is a sample of work or performance used to set the specific performance standard for a rubric level .
Perception	Perception is the process of acquiring, interpreting, selecting, and organizing sensory information.

Chapter 5. Attachment and Separation

Chapter 5. Attachment and Separation

Context	In Psychology, context refers to the background stimuli that accompany some kind of foreground event.
Guilford	Guilford observed that most individuals display a preference for either convergent or divergent thinking. Scientists and engineers typically prefer the former and artists and performers, the latter.
Separation anxiety	Separation anxiety is a psychological condition in which an individual has excessive anxiety regarding separation from home, or from those with whom the individual has a strong attachment.
Anxiety	Anxiety is a complex combination of the feeling of fear, apprehension and worry often accompanied by physical sensations such as palpitations, chest pain and/or shortness of breath.
Affect	A subjective feeling or emotional tone often accompanied by bodily expressions noticeable to others is called affect.
Sears	Sears focused on the application of the social learning theory (SLT) to socialization processes, and how children internalize the values, attitudes, and behaviors predominant in their culture. He articulated the place of parents in fostering internalization. In addition, he was among the first social learning theorists to officially acknowledge the reciprocal interaction on an individual's behavior and their environment
Society	The social sciences use the term society to mean a group of people that form a semi-closed (or semi-open) social system, in which most interactions are with other individuals belonging to the group.
Individualistic	Cultures have been classified as individualistic, which means having a set of values that give priority to personal goals rather than group goals.
Homogeneous	In biology homogeneous has a meaning similar to its meaning in mathematics. Generally it means "the same" or "of the same quality or general property".
Socialization	Social rules and social relations are created, communicated, and changed in verbal and nonverbal ways creating social complexity useful in identifying outsiders and intelligent breeding partners. The process of learning these skills is called socialization.
Child development	Scientific study of the processes of change from conception through adolescence is called child development.

Go to **Cram101.com** for the Practice Tests for this Chapter.

Chapter 5. Attachment and Separation

Chapter 6. Differing Perspectives on Learning through Play

Infancy	The developmental period that extends from birth to 18 or 24 months is called infancy.
Learning	Learning is a relatively permanent change in behavior that results from experience. Thus, to attribute a behavioral change to learning, the change must be relatively permanent and must result from experience.
Early childhood	Early childhood refers to the developmental period extending from the end of infancy to about 5 or 6 years of age; sometimes called the preschool years.
Socialization	Social rules and social relations are created, communicated, and changed in verbal and nonverbal ways creating social complexity useful in identifying outsiders and intelligent breeding partners. The process of learning these skills is called socialization.
Solitary play	Solitary Play is playing separately from others, with no reference to what others are doing
Montessori	As an educational approach, the Montessori method's central focus is on the needs, talents, gifts, and special individuality of each child. Montessori practitioners believe children learn best in their own way at their own pace.
Attention	Attention is the cognitive process of selectively concentrating on one thing while ignoring other things. Psychologists have labeled three types of attention: sustained attention, selective attention, and divided attention.
Primary color	A primary color cannot be created by mixing other colors in the gamut of a given color space.
Temperament	Temperament refers to a basic, innate disposition to change behavior. The activity level is an important dimension of temperament.
Meditation	Meditation usually refers to a state in which the body is consciously relaxed and the mind is allowed to become calm and focused.
Collective unconscious	Collective unconscious is a term of analytical psychology, originally coined by Carl Jung. It refers to that part of a person's unconscious which is common to all human beings. It contains archetypes, which are forms or symbols that are manifested by all people in all cultures.
Dramatic play	Dramatic play refers to play in which children enact social roles.
Affect	A subjective feeling or emotional tone often accompanied by bodily expressions noticeable to others is called affect.
Perception	Perception is the process of acquiring, interpreting, selecting, and organizing sensory information.
Attitude	An enduring mental representation of a person, place, or thing that evokes an emotional response and related behavior is called attitude.
Modeling	A type of behavior learned through observation of others demonstrating the same behavior is modeling.
Bias	A bias is a prejudice in a general or specific sense, usually in the sense for having a preference to one particular point of view or ideological perspective.
Nonverbal communication	Communication between individuals that does not involve the content of spoken language, but relies instead on an unspoken language of facial expressions, eye contact, and body language is nonverbal communication.
Context	In Psychology, context refers to the background stimuli that accompany some kind of foreground event.
Cognitive development	The process by which a child's understanding of the world changes as a function of age and experience is called cognitive development.

Chapter 6. Differing Perspectives on Learning through Play

Chapter 6. Differing Perspectives on Learning through Play

Individualistic	Cultures have been classified as individualistic, which means having a set of values that give priority to personal goals rather than group goals.
Developmentally appropriate practice	Education that focuses on the typical developmental patterns of children and the uniqueness of each child is called developmentally appropriate practice.
Socioeconomic	Socioeconomic pertains to the study of the social and economic impacts of any product or service offering, market intervention or other activity on an economy as a whole and on the companies, organization and individuals who are its main economic actors.
Society	The social sciences use the term society to mean a group of people that form a semi-closed (or semi-open) social system, in which most interactions are with other individuals belonging to the group.
Anchor	An anchor is a sample of work or performance used to set the specific performance standard for a rubric level.

Chapter 7. Socialization, Guidance, and Discipline

Socialization	Social rules and social relations are created, communicated, and changed in verbal and nonverbal ways creating social complexity useful in identifying outsiders and intelligent breeding partners. The process of learning these skills is called socialization.
Attachment	Attachment is the tendency to seek closeness to another person and feel secure when that person is present.
Individualism	Individualism refers to putting personal goals ahead of group goals and defining one's identity in terms of personal attributes rather than group memberships.
Individual differences	Individual differences psychology studies the ways in which individual people differ in their behavior. This is distinguished from other aspects of psychology in that although psychology is ostensibly a study of individuals, modern psychologists invariably study groups.
Society	The social sciences use the term society to mean a group of people that form a semi-closed (or semi-open) social system, in which most interactions are with other individuals belonging to the group.
Toddler	A toddler is a child between the ages of one and three years old. During this period, the child learns a great deal about social roles and develops motor skills; to toddle is to walk unsteadily.
Individualistic	Cultures have been classified as individualistic, which means having a set of values that give priority to personal goals rather than group goals.
Perception	Perception is the process of acquiring, interpreting, selecting, and organizing sensory information.
Early childhood	Early childhood refers to the developmental period extending from the end of infancy to about 5 or 6 years of age; sometimes called the preschool years.
Learning	Learning is a relatively permanent change in behavior that results from experience. Thus, to attribute a behavioral change to learning, the change must be relatively permanent and must result from experience.
Kagan	The work of Kagan supports the concept of an inborn, biologically based temperamental predisposition to severe anxiety.
Emotion	An emotion is a mental states that arise spontaneously, rather than through conscious effort. They are often accompanied by physiological changes.
Ecstasy	Ecstasy as an emotion is to be outside oneself, in a trancelike state in which an individual transcends ordinary consciousness and as a result has a heightened capacity for exceptional thought or experience. Ecstasy also refers to a relatively new hallucinogen that is chemically similar to mescaline and the amphetamines.
Punishment	Punishment is the addtion of a stimulus that reduces the frequency of a response, or the removal of a stimulus that results in a reduction of the response.
Attention	Attention is the cognitive process of selectively concentrating on one thing while ignoring other things. Psychologists have labeled three types of attention: sustained attention, selective attention, and divided attention.
Locus of control	The place to which an individual attributes control over the receiving of reinforcers -either inside or outside the self is referred to as locus of control.
Insight	Insight refers to a sudden awareness of the relationships among various elements that had previously appeared to be independent of one another.
Feedback	Feedback refers to information returned to a person about the effects a response has had.
Attitude	An enduring mental representation of a person, place, or thing that evokes an emotional

Chapter 7. Socialization, Guidance, and Discipline

Chapter 7. Socialization, Guidance, and Discipline

	response and related behavior is called attitude.
Context	In Psychology, context refers to the background stimuli that accompany some kind of foreground event.
Socioeconomic	Socioeconomic pertains to the study of the social and economic impacts of any product or service offering, market intervention or other activity on an economy as a whole and on the companies, organization and individuals who are its main economic actors.
Gender role	A cluster of behaviors that characterizes traditional female or male behaviors within a cultural setting is a gender role.
Subculture	As understood in sociology, anthropology and cultural studies, a subculture is a set of people with a distinct set of behavior and beliefs that differentiate them from a larger culture of which they are a part.
Cultural values	The importance and desirability of various objects and activities as defined by people in a given culture are referred to as cultural values.
Developmentally appropriate practice	Education that focuses on the typical developmental patterns of children and the uniqueness of each child is called developmentally appropriate practice.
Anchor	An anchor is a sample of work or performance used to set the specific performance standard for a rubric level .
Personality	Personality refers to the pattern of enduring characteristics that differentiates a person, the patterns of behaviors that make each individual unique.
Longitudinal study	Longitudinal study is a type of developmental study in which the same group of participants is followed and measured for an extended period of time, often years.
Assertiveness	Assertiveness basically means the ability to express your thoughts and feelings in a way that clearly states your needs and keeps the lines of communication open with the other.
Egocentrism	The inability to distinguish between one's own perspective and someone else's is referred to as egocentrism.
Child abuse	Child abuse is the physical or psychological maltreatment of a child.

Go to **Cram101.com** for the Practice Tests for this Chapter.

Chapter 7. Socialization, Guidance, and Discipline

Go to **Cram101.com** for the Practice Tests for this Chapter.
And, **NEVER** highlight a book again!

CPSIA information can be obtained at www.ICGtesting.com
Printed in the USA
BVOW06s1631230614

357009BV00002B/29/A